August Wilson

August Wilson is the author of *Jitney, Ma Rainey's Black
Bottom, Fences, Joe Turner's Come and Gone, The Piano
Lesson, Two Trains Running, Seven Guitars* and *King
Hedley II*. These works explore the heritage and experience of African-Americans, decade-by-decade, over the
course of the twentieth century. His plays have been pro-
duced at regional theatres across the country and all over
the world, as well as on Broadway.

Mr. Wilson's work has garnered many awards, including
Pulitzer Prizes for *Fences* (1987) and *The Piano Lesson*
(1990), a Tony Award for *Fences*, as well as seven New
York Drama Critics Circle Awards for *Ma Rainey's Black
Bottom, Fences, Joe Turner's Come and Gone, The Piano
Lesson, Two Trains Running, Seven Guitars* and *Jitney*.
Additionally, Mr. Wilson has received Rockefeller and
Guggenheim Fellowships in Playwrighting, The Whiting
Writers' Award, was awarded a 1999 National Humanities
Medal by the President of the United States, and has
received numerous honorary degrees from colleges and
universities, as well as the only high school diploma ever

issued by the Carnegie Library of Pittsburgh. He is an alumnus of New Dramatists, a member of the American Academy of Arts and Sciences, and in 1995 he was inducted into the American Academy of Arts and Letters.

Mr. Wilson serves as Chairman of the Board for the African Grove Institute for the Arts (AGIA). The formation of AGIA heeded the call made in the speech "The Ground on Which I Stand." AGIA is dedicated to creating an environment to support artistic excellence and to promote the advancement and preservation of Black Theatre and Black Performing Arts.

Mr. Wilson was born and raised in the Hill District of Pittsburgh, Pennsylvania, and currently makes his home in Seattle, Washington. He is the father of two daughters, Sakina Ansari and Azula Carmen Wilson, and is married to costume designer Constanza Romero.

THE GROUND
ON WHICH I STAND

August Wilson

THE GROUND
ON WHICH I STAND

THEATRE COMMUNICATIONS GROUP
New York

The Ground on Which I Stand is published by Theatre Communications
Group, Inc., 520 Eighth Avenue, 24th Floor, New York, NY 10018-4156.

The Dramatic Contexts series is published in arrangement with Nick Hern
Books Limited, The Glasshouse, 49a Goldhawk Road, Shepherd's Bush,
London, England W12 8QP.

This publication is made possible in part with public funds from the New York
State Council on the Arts, a State Agency.

TCG books are exclusively distributed to the book trade by Consortium Book
Sales and Distribution, 1045 Westgate Drive, St. Paul, MN 55114.

Library of Congress Cataloging-in-Publication Data

Wilson, August.
The ground on which I stand / by August Wilson. — 1st ed.
p. cm. — (Dramatic contexts)
Address originally delivered June 26, 1996 to the 11th biennial Theatre
Communications Group National Conference at Princeton University.
ISBN-13: 978-1-55936-187-3
ISBN-10: 1-55936-187-5
1. American drama—Afro-American authors—History and criticism. 2. Afro-
American theater—History. 3. American drama—20th century—History and
criticism. 4. Theater and society—United States—History—20th century.
5. Afro-Americans in literature.
I. Title. II. Series.
PS338.N4 W55 2000
812'.5409896073—dc21 00-037805

First Edition, September 2001
Third Printing, January 2011

Playwright August Wilson delivered this address June 26, 1996, to the 11th biennial Theatre Communications Group National Conference at Princeton University.

THE GROUND ON WHICH I STAND

Some time ago I had an occasion to speak to a group of international playwrights. They had come from all over the world—from Colombia, Chile, from New Guinea, Poland, China, Nigeria, Italy, France, Great Britain. I began my remarks by welcoming them to my country. I didn't always think of it as my country, but since my ancestors have been here since the early seventeenth century, I thought it as good a beginning as any. So I say if there are any foreigners here in the audience, welcome to my country.

I wish to make it clear from the outset that I do not have a mandate to speak for anyone. There are many intelligent blacks working in the American theatre who speak in a loud and articulate voice. It would be the greatest of presumptions to say that I speak for them. I speak only for myself and those who may think as I do.

I have come here today to make a testimony, to talk about the ground on which I stand and all the many grounds on which I and my ancestors have toiled, and the ground of theatre on which my fellow artists and I have labored to bring forth its fruits, its daring and its sometimes lacerating, and often healing, truths.

The first and most obvious ground I am standing on is this platform, that I have so graciously been given at the 11th biennial conference of the Theatre Communications Group. It is the Theatre Communications Group to which we owe much of our organization and communication, and I am grateful to them for entrusting me with the grave responsibility of sounding this keynote, and it is my hope to discharge my duties faithfully. I first attended the conference in 1984, and I recall John Hirsch's eloquent address on the "Other" and I mark it as a moment of enlightenment and import. And I am proud and thankful to stand here tonight in my embrace of that moment and to find myself on this platform. It is a moment I count well and mark with privilege.

In one guise, the ground I stand on has been pioneered by the Greek dramatists—by Euripides, Aeschylus and Sophocles—by William Shakespeare, by Shaw, Ibsen and Chekov, Eugene O'Neill, Arthur Miller, Tennessee Williams. In another guise, the ground that I stand on has been pioneered by my grandfather, by Nat Turner, by Denmark Vesey, by Martin Delaney, Marcus Garvey and the Honorable Elijah Muhammad. That is the ground of the affirmation of the value of one's being, an affirmation of his worth in the face of this society's urgent and some-times profound denial. It was this ground as a young man coming into manhood searching for something to dedicate my life to that I discovered the Black Power Movement of the '60s. I felt it a duty and an honor to participate in that historic moment. As a people who had arrived in America chained and malnourished in the hold of a 350-foot Portuguese, Dutch or English sailing ship, we were now seeking ways to alter our relationship to the society in which we live—and, perhaps more important, searching for ways to alter the shared expectations of ourselves as a community of people.

I find it curious but no small accident that I seldom hear those words "Black Power" spoken, and when mention is made of that part of black history in America, whether in the press or in conversation, reference is made to the Civil Rights Movement as though the Black Power Movement—an important social movement by America's ex-slaves—had in fact never happened. But the Black Power Movement of the '60s was [in fact] a reality; it was the kiln in which I was fired, and has much to do with the person I am today and the ideas and attitudes that I carry as part of my consciousness.

I mention this because it is difficult to disassociate my concerns with theatre from the concerns of my life as a black man, and it is difficult to disassociate one part of my life from another. I have strived to live it all seamless—art and life together, inseparable and indistinguishable. The ideas I discovered and embraced in my youth when my idealism was full blown I have not abandoned in middle age when idealism is something less than blooming, but wisdom is starting to bud. The ideas of self-determination, self-respect and self-defense that governed my life in the '60s I find just as valid and self-urging in 1996. The need to alter our relationship to the society and to alter the shared expectations of ourselves as a racial group I find of greater urgency now than it was then.

I am what is known, at least among the

followers and supporters of the ideas of Marcus Garvey, as a "race man." That is simply that I believe that race matters—that is the largest, most identifiable and most important part of our personality. It is the largest category of identification because it is the one that most influences your perception of yourself, and it is the one to which others in the world of men most respond. Race is also an important part of the American landscape, as America is made up of an amalgamation of races from all parts of the globe. Race is also the product of a shared gene pool that allows for group identification, and it is an organizing principle around which cultures are formed. When I say culture I am speaking about the behavior patterns, the arts, beliefs, institutions and all other products of human work and thought as expressed by a particular community of people.

There are some people who will say that black Americans do not have a culture—that cultures are reserved for other people, most notably Europeans of various ethnic groupings, and that black Americans make up a sub-group of American culture that is derived from the European origins of its majority population. But black Americans are Africans, and there are many histories and many cultures on the African continent.

Those who would deny black Americans their culture would also deny them their history and the inherent values that are a part of all human life.

Growing up in my mother's house at 1727 Bedford Avenue in Pittsburgh, PA, I learned the language, the eating habits, the religious beliefs, the gestures, the notions of common sense, attitudes towards sex, concepts of beauty and justice, and the responses to pleasure and pain...that my mother had learned from her mother, and which you could trace back to the first African who set foot on the continent. It is this culture that stands today on these shores today as a testament to the resiliency of the African-American spirit.

The term black or African-American not only denotes race, it denotes condition, and carries with it the vestige of slavery and the social segregation and abuse of opportunity so vivid in our memory. That this abuse of opportunity and truncation of possibility is continuing and is so pervasive in our society in 1996 says much about who we are and much about the work that is necessary to alter our perceptions of each other and to effect meaningful prosperity for all.

The problematic nature of the relationship between whites and blacks has for too long led us astray from the fulfillment of our possibilities as a society. We stare at each other across a divide of economics and privilege that has become an encumbrance on black Americans' ability to prosper and on the collective will and spirit of our national purpose.

I speak about economics and privilege, one significant fact affects us all in the American theatre: of the sixty-six LORT theatres, there is one that can be considered black. From this it could be falsely assumed that there aren't sufficient numbers of blacks working in the American theatre to sustain and support more theatres.

If you do not know, I will tell you: black theatre in America is alive, it is vibrant, it is vital...it just isn't funded.

Black theatre doesn't share in the economics that would allow it to support its artists and supply them with meaningful avenues to develop their talent and broadcast and disseminate ideas crucial to its growth. The economics are reserved as privilege to the overwhelming abundance of institutions that preserve, promote and perpetuate white culture.

That is not a complaint. That is an advertisement. Since the funding sources, both public and private, do not publicly carry avowed missions of exclusion and segregated support, this is obviously either a glaring case of oversight, or we the proponents of black theatre have not made our presence or our needs known. I hope here tonight to correct both of those oversights and assumptions.

I do not have the time in this short talk to reiterate the long and distinguished history of black theatre—often accomplished amid adverse and hostile conditions—but I would like to take the time to mark a few high points.

There are and have always been two distinct and parallel traditions in black art: that is, art that is conceived and designed to entertain white society, and art that feeds the spirit and celebrates the life of black America by designing its strategies for survival and prosperity.

An important part of black theatre that is often ignored but is seminal to its tradition is its origins on the slave plantations of the South. Summoned to the "big house" to entertain the slave owner and his guests, the slave began a tradition of theatre as entertainment for whites that reached its pinnacle in the heyday of the Harlem Renaissance. This entertainment for whites consisted of whatever the slave imagined or knew that his master wanted to see and hear. This tradition has its present-life counterpart in the crossover artists that slant their material for white consumption.

The second tradition occurred when the African in the confines of the slave quarters sought to invest his spirit with the strength of his ancestors by conceiving in his art, in his song and dance, a world in which he was the spiritual center, and his existence was a manifest act of the creator from whom life flowed. He could then create art that was functional and furnished him with a spiritual temperament necessary for his survival as property and the dehumanizing status that was attendant to that.

I stand myself and my art squarely on the self-defining ground of the slave quarters, and find the ground to be hallowed and made fertile by the blood and bones of the men and women who can be described as warriors on the cultural battlefield that affirmed their self-worth. As there is no idea that cannot be contained by black life, these men and women found themselves to be sufficient and secure in their art and their instructions.

It was this high ground of self-determination that the black playwrights of the '60s marked out for themselves. Ron Milner; Ed Bullins; Philip Hayes Dean; Richard Wesley; Lonne Elder, III; Sonia Sanchez; Barbara Ann Teer and Amiri Baraka were among those playwrights who were particularly vocal and whose talents confirmed their presence in the society, and altered the American theatre, its meaning, its craft and its history. This brilliant explosion of black arts and letters in the '60s remains for me the hallmark and the signpost that points the way to our contemporary work on the same ground. Black playwrights everywhere remain indebted to them for their brave and courageous forays into an area that is marked with land mines and the shadows of snipers—those who would reserve the territory of arts and letters and the American theatre as their own special province and point blacks toward the ball fields and the bandstands.

That black theatre today comes under such assaults should surprise no one, as we are on the verge of reclaiming and reexamining the purpose and pillars of our art and laying out new directions for its expansion. And as such we make a target for cultural imperialists who seek to empower and propagate their ideas about the world as the only valid ideas, and see blacks as woefully deficient not only in arts and letters but in the abundant gifts of humanity.

In the nineteenth century, the lack of education, the lack of contact with different cultures, the expensive and slow methods of travel and communication fostered such ideas, and the breeding ground of ignorance and racial intolerance promoted them.

The King's English and the lexicon of a people given to such ignorance and intolerance did not do much to dispel such obvious misconceptions, but provided them with a home. I cite *Webster's Third New International Dictionary*:

> "BLACK: outrageously wicked, dishonorable, connected with the devil, menacing, sullen, hostile, unqualified, illicit, illegal, violators of public regulations, affected by some undesirable condition..." etc.

> "WHITE: free from blemish, moral stain or impurity; outstandingly righteous, innocent; not marked by

malignant influence; notably auspicious, fortunate, decent; a sterling man."

Such is the linguistic environment that informs the distance that separates blacks and whites in America and which the cultural imperialists, who cannot imagine a life existing and flourishing outside their benevolent control, embraces.

Robert Brustein, writing in an article/review titled "Unity from Diversity" [*The New Republic*, July 19–26, 1993], is apparently disturbed that "there is a tremendous outpouring of work by minority artists" which he attributes to cultural diversity. He writes that the practice of extending invitations to a national banquet from which a lot of hungry people have long been excluded is a practice that can lead to confused standards. He goes on to establish a presumption of inferiority of the work of minority artists: "Funding agencies have started substituting sociological criteria for aesthetic criteria in their grant procedures, indicating that 'elitist' notions like quality and excellence are no longer functional." He goes on to say: "It's disarming in all senses of the word to say that we don't share common experiences that are measurable by common standards. But the growing number of truly talented artists with more universal interests suggests that we may soon be in a position to return to a single value system."

Brustein's surprisingly sophomoric assumption that this tremendous outpouring of work by minority artists leads to confusing standards and that funding agencies have started substituting sociological for aesthetic criteria, leaving aside notions like quality and excellence, shows him to be a victim of nineteenth-century thinking and the linguistic environment that posits blacks as unqualified. Quite possibly this tremendous outpouring of works by minority artists may lead to a *raising* of standards and a *raising* of the levels of excellence, but Mr. Brustein cannot allow that possibility.

To suggest that funding agencies are rewarding inferior work by pursuing sociological criteria only serves to call into question the tremendous outpouring of plays by white playwrights who benefit from funding given to the sixty-six LORT theatres.

Are those theatres funded on sociological or aesthetic criteria? Do we have sixty-six excellent theatres? Or do those theatres benefit from the sociological advantage that they are run by whites and cater to largely white audiences?

The truth is that often where there are aesthetic criteria of excellence, it is the sociological criteria that have traditionally excluded blacks. I say raise the standards and remove the sociological conditions of race as privilege, and we will meet you at the crossroads, in equal numbers, prepared to do the work of extending and developing the common ground of the American theatre.

We are capable of work of the highest order; we can answer to the high standards of world-class art. And anyone who doubts our capabilities at this late stage is being intellectually dishonest.

We can meet on the common ground of theatre as a field of work and endeavor. But we cannot meet on the common ground of experience.

Where is the common ground in the horrifics of lynching? Where is the common ground in the maim of the policeman's bullet? Where is the common ground in the hull of a slave ship or the deck of a slave ship with its refreshments of air and expanse?

We will not be denied our history.

We have voice and we have temper. We are too far along this road from the loss of our political will, we are too far along the road of reassembling ourselves, too far along the road to regaining spiritual health to allow such transgression of our history to go unchallenged.

The commonalties that we share are the commonalities of culture. We decorate our houses. That is something we do in common. We do it differently because we value different things. We have different manners and different values of social intercourse. We have different ideas of what a party is.

There are some commonalities to our different ideas. We both offer food and drink to our guests, but because we have different culinary values, different culinary histories, we offer different food and drink to our guests. As an example, in our culinary history, we have learned to make do with the feet and ears and tails and intestines of the pig rather than the loin and the ham and the bacon. Because of our different histories with the same animal, we have different culinary ideas. But we share a common experience with the pig as opposed to say Muslims and Jews, who do not share that experience.

We can meet on the common ground of the American theatre.

We cannot share a single value system if that value system consists of the values of white Americans based on their European ancestors. We reject that as Cultural Imperialism. We need a value system that includes our contributions as Africans in America. Our agendas are as valid as yours. We may disagree, we may forever be on opposite sides of aesthetics, but we can only share a value system that is inclusive of all Americans and recognizes their unique and valuable contributions.

The ground together: We must develop the ground together. We reject the idea of equality among equals, but we say rather the equality of all men.

The common values of the American theatre that we can share are plot...dialogue...characterization...design. How we both make use of them will be determined by who we are and what ground we are standing on and what our cultural values are.

Theatre is part of art history in terms of its craft and dramaturgy, but it is part of social history in terms of how it is financed and governed. By making money available to theatres willing to support colorblind casting, the financiers and governors have signaled not only their unwillingness to support black theatre but their willingness to fund dangerous and divisive assaults against it. Colorblind casting is an aberrant idea that has never had any validity other than as a tool of the Cultural Imperialists who view their American culture, rooted in the icons of European culture, as beyond reproach in its perfection. It is inconceivable to them that life could be lived and enriched without knowing Shakespeare or Mozart. Their gods, their manners, their being, are the only true and correct representations of humankind. They refuse to recognize black conduct and manners as part of a system that is fueled by its own philosophy, mythology, history, creative motif, social organization and ethos. The idea that blacks have their own way of responding to the world, their own values, style, linguistics, their own religion and aesthetics, is unacceptable to them.

For a black actor to stand on the stage as part of a social milieu that has denied him his gods, his culture, his humanity, his mores, his ideas of himself and the world he lives in, is to be in league with a thousand naysayers who wish to corrupt the vigor and spirit of his heart.

To cast us in the role of mimics is to deny us our own competence.

Our manners, our style, our approach to language, our gestures, and our bodies are not for rent. The history of our bodies—the maimings, the lashings, the lynchings, the body that is capable of inspiring profound rage and pungent cruelty—is not for rent. Nor is the meaning of our history or our bodies for rent.

To mount an all-black production of a

Death of a Salesman or any other play conceived for white actors as an investigation of the human condition through the specifics of white culture is to deny us our own humanity, our own history, and the need to make our own investigations from the cultural ground on which we stand as black Americans. It is an assault on our presence, and our difficult but honorable history in America; and it is an insult to our intelligence, our playwrights, and our many and varied contributions to the society and the world at large.

The idea of colorblind casting is the same idea of assimilation that black Americans have been rejecting for the past 380 years. For the record, we reject it again. We reject any attempt to blot us out, to reinvent our history and ignore our presence or to maim our spiritual product. We must not continue to meet on this path. We will not deny our history, and we will not allow it to be made to be of little consequence, to be ignored or misinterpreted.

In an effort to spare us the burden of being "affected by an undesirable condition" and as a gesture of benevolence, many whites (like the proponents of colorblind casting) say, "Oh, I don't see color." We want you to see us. We are black and beautiful. We are not patrons of the linguistic environment that would have us as "unqualified," and "violators of public regulations." We are not ashamed. We have an honorable history in the world of men. We come from a long line of honorable people with complex codes of ethics and social discourse, who devised myths and systems of cosmology and systems of economics, and who were themselves part of a long social and political history. We are not ashamed, and we do not need you to be ashamed for us. Nor do we need the recognition of our blackness to be couched in abstract phases like "artist of color." Who are you talking about? A Japanese artist? An Eskimo? A Filipino? A Mexican? A Cambodian? A Nigerian? Are we to suppose

that one white person balances out the rest
of humanity lumped together as nondescript
"people of color"? We reject that. We are
unique, and we are specific.

W e do not need colorblind casting;
we need theatres. We need theatres to develop our playwrights.
We need those misguided financial resources
to be put to better use. Without theatres we
cannot develop our talents. If we cannot
develop our talents, then everyone suffers:
our writers, the theatre, the audience. Actors
are deprived of material, and our communi-
ties are deprived of the jobs in support of the
art—the company manager, the press coordi-
nator, the electricians, the carpenters, the
concessionaires, the people that work in
wardrobe, the box-office staff, the ushers and
the janitors. We need some theatres. We have
only one life to develop our talent, to fulfill
our potential as artists. One life, and it is
short, and the lack of the means to develop

our talent is an encumbrance on that life.

We did not sit on the sidelines while the immigrants of Europe, through hard work, skill, cunning, guile and opportunity, built America into an industrial giant of the twentieth century. It was our labor that provided the capital. It was our labor in the shipyards and the stockyards and the coal mines and the steel mills. Our labor built the roads and the railroads. And when America was challenged, we strode on the battlefield, our boots strapped on and our blood left to soak into the soil of places whose names we could not pronounce, against an enemy whose only crime was ideology. We left our blood in France and Korea and the Philippines and Vietnam, and our only reward has been the deprivation of possibility and the denial of our moral personality.

It cannot continue. The ground together: The American ground on which I stand and which my ancestors purchased with their perseverance, with their survival, with their manners and with their faith.

It cannot continue, as well as other assaults upon our presence and our history cannot continue: When the *New York Times* publishes an article on pop singer Michael Bolton and lists as his influences four white singers, and then as an afterthought tosses in the phrase "and the great black rhythm and blues singers," it cannot be anything but purposeful with intent to maim. These great black rhythm and blues singers are reduced to an afterthought on the verge of oblivion—one stroke of the editor's pen and the history of American music is revised, and Otis Redding, Jerry Butler and Rufus Thomas are consigned to the dustbin of history while Joe Cocker, Mick Jagger and Rod Stewart are elevated to the status of the originators and creators of a vital art that is a product of our spiritual travails; and the history of music becomes a fabrication, a blatant forgery which under the hallowed auspices of the *New York Times* is presented as the genuine article.

We cannot accept these assaults. We must defend and protect our spiritual fruits. To ignore these assaults would make us derelict in our duties. We cannot accept them. Our political capital will not permit them.

So much of what makes this country rich in art and all manners of spiritual life is the contributions that we as African Americans have made. We cannot allow others to have authority over our cultural and spiritual products. We reject, without reservation, any attempt by anyone to rewrite our history so as to deny us the rewards of our spiritual labors, and to become the cultural custodians of our art, our literature and our lives. To give expression to the spirit that has been shaped and fashioned by our history is of necessity to give voice and vent to the history itself.

It must remain for us a history of triumph.

The time has come for black playwrights to confer with one another, to come together to meet each other face to face, to address questions of aesthetics and ways to defend ourselves from the naysayers who would trumpet our talents as insufficient to warrant the same manner of investigation and exploration as the majority. We need to develop guidelines for the protection of our cultural property, our contributions and the influence they accrue. It is time we took the responsibility for our talents in our own hands. We cannot depend on others. We cannot depend on the directors, the managers or the actors to do the work we should be doing for ourselves. It is our lives, our talent and the pursuit of our fulfillment that are being encumbered by false ideas and perceptions of ourselves.

It is time to embrace the political dictates of our history and answer the challenge to our duties. And I further think we should confer in a city in our ancestral homeland in the southern part of the United States in 1998, so that we may enter the millennium united and prepared for a long future of prosperity.

From the hull of a ship to self-determining, self-respecting people. That is the journey we are making.

We are robust in spirit, we are bright with laughter, and we are bold in imagination. Our blood is soaked into the soil and our bones lie scattered the whole way across the Atlantic Ocean, as Hansel's crumbs, to mark our way back home.

We are no longer in the House of Bondage, and soon we will no longer be victims of the counting houses who hold from us ways to develop and support our talents and our expressions of life and its varied meanings. Assaults upon the body politic that demean and ridicule and depress the value and worth of our existence, that seek to render it immobile and to extinguish the flame of freedom lit eons ago by our ancestors upon another continent, must be met with a fierce and uncompromising defense.

If you are willing to accept it, it is your duty to affirm and urge that defense, and that respect and that determination.

And I must mention here, with all due respect to W. E. B. DuBois, that the concept of a "talented tenth" creates an artificial superiority. It is a fallacy and a dangerous idea that only serves to divide us further. I am not willing to throw away as untalented ninety percent of my blood; I am not willing to dismiss the sons and daughters of those people who gave more than lip service to the will to live and made it a duty to prosper in spirit, if not in provision. All God's children got talent. It is a dangerous idea to set one part of the populace above and aside from the other. We do a grave disservice to ourselves not to seek out and embrace and enable all of our human resources as a people. All blacks in America, with very few exceptions—*with very few exceptions*—no matter what our status, no matter the size of our bank accounts, no matter how many and what kind of academic degrees we can place beside our names, no matter the furnishings and square footage of our homes, the length of our closets and the quality of the wool and cotton that hangs there—we all in America originated from the same place: the slave plantations of the South. We all share a common past, and despite how some of us might think and how it might look, we all share a common present and will share a common future.

We can make a difference. Artists, playwrights, actors—we can be the spearhead of a movement to reignite and reunite our people's positive energy for a political and social change that is reflective of our spiritual truths rather than economic fallacies. Our talents, our truths, our belief in ourselves is all in our hands. What we make of it will emerge from the self as a baptismal spray that names and defines. What we do now becomes history by which our grandchildren will judge us.

We are not off on a tangent. The foundation of the American theatre is the foundation of European theatre that begins with the great Greek dramatists; it is based on the proscenium stage and the poetics of Aristotle. This is the theatre that we have chosen to work in. And we embrace the values of that theatre but reserve the right to amend, to explore, and to add our African consciousness and our African aesthetic to the art we produce.

To pursue our cultural expression does not separate us. We are not separatists, as Mr. Brustein asserts. We are Americans trying to fulfill our talents. We are not the servants at the party. We are not apprentices in the kitchens. We are not the stable boys to the king's huntsmen. We are Africans. We are Americans. The irreversible sweep of history has decreed that. We are artists who seek to develop our talents and give expression to our personalities. We bring advantage to the common ground that is the American theatre.

All theatres depend on an audience for a dialogue. To the American theatre, subscription audiences are its life blood. But the subscription audience holds theatres hostage to the mediocrity of its tastes, and impedes the further development of an audience for the work that we do. While intentional or not, it serves to keep blacks out of the theatre. A subscription audience becomes not a support system but makes the patrons members of a club to which the theatre serves as a clubhouse. It is an irony that the people who can most afford a full-price ticket get discounts for subscribing, while the single-ticket buyer who cannot afford a subscription is charged the additional burden of support to offset the subscription-buyer's discount. It is a system that is in need of overhaul to provide not only a more equitable access to tickets but access to influence as well.

I look for and challenge students of arts management to be bold in their exploration of new systems of funding theatres, including profit-making institutions and ventures, and I challenge black artists and audiences to scale the walls erected by theatre subscriptions to gain access to this vital area of spiritual enlightenment and enrichment that is the theatre.

All theatregoers have opinions about the work they witness. Critics have an informed opinion. Sometimes it may be necessary for them to gather more information to become more informed. As playwrights grow and develop, as the theatre changes, the critic has an important responsibility to guide and encourage that growth. However, in the discharge of their duties, it may be necessary for them to also grow and develop. A stagnant body of critics, operating from the critical criteria of forty years ago, makes for a stagnant theatre without the fresh and abiding influence of contemporary ideas. It is the critics who should be in the forefront of developing new tools for analysis necessary to understand new influences.

The critic who can recognize a German neo-romantic influence should also be able to recognize an American influence from blues or black church rituals, or any other contemporary American influence.

The true critic does not sit in judgment. Rather he seeks to inform his reader, instead of adopting a posture of self-conscious importance in which he sees himself a judge and final arbiter of a work's importance or value.

We stand on the verge of an explosion of playwriting talent that will challenge our critics. As American playwrights absorb the influence of television and use new avenues of approach to the practice of their craft, they will grow to be wildly inventive and imaginative in creating dramas that will guide and influence contemporary life for years to come.

Theatre can do that. It can disseminate ideas, it can educate even the miseducated, because it is art—and all art reaches across that divide that makes order out of chaos, and embraces the truth that overwhelms with its presence, and connects man to something larger than himself and his imagination.

Theatre asserts that all of human life is universal. Love, Honor, Duty, Betrayal belong and pertain to every culture and every race. The way they are acted out on the playing field may be different, but betrayal is betrayal whether you are a South Sea Islander, a Mississippi farmer or an English baron. All of human life is universal, and it is theatre that illuminates and confers upon the universal the ability to speak for all men.

The ground together: We have to do it together. We cannot permit our lives to waste away, our talents unchallenged. We cannot permit a failure to our duty. We are brave and we are boisterous, our mettle is proven, and we are dedicated.

The ground together: the ground of the American theatre on which I am proud to

stand...the ground which our artistic ancestors purchased with their endeavors...with
their pursuit of the American spirit and its
ideals.

I believe in the American theatre. I
believe in its power to inform about the
human condition, I believe in its power to
heal, "to hold the mirror as 'twere up to
nature," to the truths we uncover, to the
truths we wrestle from uncertain and some-
times unyielding realities. All of art is a
search for ways of being, of living life more
fully. We who are capable of those noble pur-
suits should challenge the melancholy and
barbaric, to bring the light of angelic grace,
peace, prosperity and the unencumbered
pursuit of happiness to the ground on which
we all stand. Thank you.

Other Dramatic Contexts titles include:

Evoking Shakespeare
by Peter Brook

The Necessary Theatre
by Peter Hall

Poetics
by Aristotle
translated by Kenneth McLeish